Finding Out About
VICTORIAN
COUNTRY LIFE

Michael Rawcliffe

Batsford Academic and Educational   *London*

—•—Contents —•—

Introduction	3
Useful Sources	4
The Country Town	6
The Village	8
Estate Villages	10
The Cottage	12
The Country House	14
The Estate Owner	16
The Village Church	18
Working on the Land	20
Working in the Woods	22
Rural Gangs	24
Children at Work	26
Hops and Hop Picking	28
Harvest Time	30
Country Crafts	32
Inns and Fairs	34
Upper-Class Leisure	36
The Country School	38
Budgets and Diets	40
Transport	42
Difficult Words	45
Places to Visit	46
Biographical Notes	47
Book List	47
Index	48

Typeset by Tek-Art Ltd, Kent
and printed in Spain by
Grijelmo SA, Bilbao
for the publishers
Batsford Academic and Educational,
an imprint of B. T. Batsford Ltd,
4 Fitzhardinge Street
London W1H 0AH

ISBN 0 7134 4351 0

ACKNOWLEDGMENTS

The Author and Publishers would like to thank
the following for their permission to reproduce
illustrations: the Institute of Agricultural
History and Museum of English Rural Life,
University of Reading, page 12; Kent Archives
Office, pages 16 (Cat. Mark U310 A108), 36 (Cat.
Mark U951 F30/1). The diagrams on pages 11
and 29 were drawn by R.F. Brien. The map on
page 44 was drawn by Rudolph Britto. The
illustrations on pages 5, 10, 15, 23, 28, 29, 37
and 41 are in the Author's collection.

Introduction

This book is about the countryside during the reign of Queen Victoria, 1837-1901. Today, most of us live in towns and cities. This was not always so and it was not until 1851 that the number of people living in the countryside was equalled by town dwellers. By this time, 6,000 miles of railway track had been laid, and people could travel more quickly and cheaply. Goods, food and animals could also be sent from distant parts to the growing cities. For example, from the 1860s the London milk trade was served by counties as far away as Hampshire; whilst fish, Scottish strawberries and other soft fruits could be moved many miles without danger of deterioration.

The railway was not the only source of change. By the end of the nineteenth century machinery such as steam ploughs and combine harvesters was used on the larger farms and the widespread use of fertilizers and tile drainage had enabled the land to be worked more effectively.

Improved transport enabled many to leave the land altogether, sometimes for jobs in the towns or even to make a new life in the USA, Canada, Australia or New Zealand.

Among those who stayed on the land, families who lived in quiet villages surrounding the towns might well have found them unrecognizable within their own lifetimes. Country lanes and fields soon sprouted builders' carts, "For Sale" signs and eventually houses, which were bought or rented by families in which the father probably travelled each day from the suburb into the city.

For those who still worked on the land, life gradually improved, except for those in the wheat-growing counties which, in the 1870s and '80s, faced severe competition from cheap grain imported from the Prairies. It was during this time that many farming families gave up the unequal struggle and migrated to the USA or to the Empire.

As the population grew and as the standard of living rose, so did demands for fresh meat, dairy products and soft fruit. Thus, some areas prospered even during the worst farming years.

Nevertheless, at the end of the century, several counties and country areas were still very remote and several miles from a town or from a station. Where there were still too many workers for the available jobs, wages were low and times were hard. For the old, the sick and the poor, the workhouse was the last resort. Sickness, injury or severe weather could bring disaster to a family.

This book contains many contrasts. The gentry on their estates provided work for many. They travelled widely, sent their children to boarding school and probably spent part of the year in London or abroad. At the other end of the scale were families who had been on the land for several generations, who sent their children to the village school and expected them to earn as soon as they were able. There were still some people who had not been beyond the next village and whose entertainment was the village inn and the market or fair.

By the end of the century those living in the large country houses and some in the market towns had piped water, inside lavatories, gas and even electricity. Cottagers were often still burning candles and oil lamps, drawing water from a well and using an outside toilet.

In addition, many of the village buildings were very old, even in Victorian times. People on the verge of poverty were unable to maintain them. The thatch would be overgrown with grass, or the tiles cracked, the windows and doors ill-fitting and draughty, whilst, inside, rags and sacking may have

—Useful Sources—

Village women, Barston, Warwickshire. An old building even in 1890. Note the new door and window frame, and the stables.

served as carpets. Furniture was sparse and many of the rooms were used for both eating and sleeping. Today, many of these same houses have been "done up" and the dishevelled and run-down Tudor timber-framed house transformed into an attractive property, well-maintained outside and carefully furnished inside.

Overall, great changes took place, but in 1901 there were still many people employed on the land working with their hands, spade and shovel and without machinery. The horse and human muscle were still the main features of the countryside at work.

There are many ways in which you can discover more about the Victorian countryside. Some of these are listed below.

1. PEOPLE

Very few people living today were born in Victorian times, but many old people will be able to tell you about their parents or grandparents or recall local information and stories which will be of interest to you.

When you have decided what you wish to study, the first specialist you should visit is the archivist or local history librarian at your main library. Several town libraries have their own local history section and every county has its county record office. If you live in a small town or village your local records may be there. Sections 3, 4 and 5 contain examples of sources which may be found in larger libraries. Smaller ones may not have original sources on your area. If you wish to visit the county record office, remember to write first.

2. THE VILLAGE ITSELF

Start at the Parish Church. Find out when it was built or modernized (this is often in Victorian times). Look out for memorials inside the church and at the gravestones outside. They will tell you a lot about local families. Sometimes churches are locked during the day. If so, look on the notice board for the address of the vicar, church warden or verger who will often be pleased to help.

Next find the main street or market square. Walk along it looking at houses from across the road, trying to imagine the houses without their modern shop fronts or alterations (see 3b).

3. VISUAL MATERIAL

a) *Old photographs* There are still many Victorian photographs available. Family albums may contain photographs of our Victorian ancestors dressed in their Sunday best. Original photographs of village streets, market days, harvesting, etc, are difficult to find, but several libraries and museums sell reproductions, sometimes as postcards.

b) *Maps* By the middle of the nineteenth century the Ordnance Survey had produced large-scale

A Victorian viaduct crossing the Darent Valley in Kent. Imagine the number of navvies who would have been employed in constructing it. Do you think it blends in with the landscape?

maps (6" and 25" scale) of the whole country. These were frequently brought up to date, and you will find them in your local library. It is a good idea to buy a xerox copy of the area you wish to study. The 25" scale is large enough to show the shape of every house and even individual trees and pillar boxes. You can then walk round the area noting changes which have taken place.

c) *Prints and paintings* Before the photograph, many prints were produced of local landmarks, such as churches and village streets. The local library may have examples, and also paintings by local people of the area in Victorian times.

4. WRITTEN SOURCES

In the local history library you will find the following:

a) *Local histories* These may be recent, or actually written in the nineteenth century. The latter may contain interesting illustrations and also descriptions of buildings or activities which no longer exist.

b) *Local directories* Several firms produced county directories which gave detailed descriptions of each town and village. These included the population, number of houses, names of the leading residents, the local schools, carriers and a useful trade list. *Kelly's Post Office Directory* is one of the best-known and most informative.

c) *Advertisements* Guides, directories and newspapers contain interesting advertisements which provide valuable detail about such things as local trades, inns, coach and agricultural machinery firms.

d) *Documents* These were written at the time for practical use. You may find in the library bills from the local vet, school log books, workhouse diet sheets, labour books or posters advertising local fairs.

e) *Diaries or memoirs* Libraries sometimes have diaries or memoirs written by local people, which have been left in their safekeeping. Or you may find an autobiography published by someone who lived in your area in Victorian times.

f) *Census material* The first national census was in 1801. From 1851 the census returns list useful local information about each member of the family who was in residence on census day. These include age, occupation and place of birth. Because the details are personal the census returns are not published until 100 years after they were collected. The local library may have the returns for your area on microfilm.

5. OBJECTS

The local museum may have examples of (a) fairings — literally presents which were bought at village fairs, (b) medals given to prize winners at agricultural shows or to children for punctuality and good attendance at the village school, (c) hop tokens which were given for work done and then cashed at the end of the week. In the village itself look for mounting posts, gas lamp holders, Victorian pillar boxes, well pumps and milestones.

6. ROAD, FIELD AND INN NAMES

These give us clues to the past. The market square may now be built on or reduced in area, but the name may remain. Inn names, such as the Sawyers Arms, the Hop-Pickers, the Woodman, the Drovers Arms, the Coach and Horses and the Railway Inn all tell their tale; whilst roads such as Highfield Road, Boundary Road, High Furlong Road, Tile Farm Road, may remind us of what was country a hundred years ago.

The Country Town

The typical country town in 1837 had between one and three thousand inhabitants. It served the surrounding countryside to a radius of between three and four miles and usually held a weekly market and perhaps an annual fair. It would have a few shops, small workshops, a brewery and a number of professional people such as a doctor and a solicitor.

AN ISOLATED TOWN

Whether a town developed during the nineteenth century usually depended on its position. Bampton in Devon, described in Murray's *Guide to Devon and Cornwall,* had a population of 1,928 in 1871. Note the distance to the nearest railway station.

A small secluded town embedded among hills in a singularly beautiful country. It is seven miles from Tiverton station by two roads, the new and the old but on these the only public conveyance is a van three times a week.

A TOWN IN DECLINE

Wickham Market in Suffolk had long been in decline and its lack of a station meant that its population declined between 1851 and 1871. Its population in 1871 was 1,541, according to John Wilson in his *Imperial Gazetteer of England and Wales* for 1876:

The town stands on the river Deben. Was once a place of considerable importance with a shire hall, now taken down, had formerly a weekly market and two fairs, now disused. Population 1851 – 1697, 1861 – 1571, of which 133 were in the workhouse.

Why do you think the market and fairs had ended? Do you think that this made things worse for the town?

This extract from Knight's Suffolk Almanack *for 1875 gives us a good picture of Wickham Market. Note the dependence on the carrier. How was your town served at this time?*

WICKHAM MARKET.

Solicitor.—Mr. James Pringle Barclay.

Schools.—NATIONAL, W. J. Bales and Mrs. Bales, master and mistress. MIDDLE CLASS BOARDING AND DAY, "THE LIMES" Villa; proprietor, Mr. W. Bales; resident governess, Miss A. Carter.

Suffolk Alliance Fire and Life Assurance Company.—Agent, Mr. W. Whitmore.

Wickham Market Gas Company Limited.—C. H. Read, secretary and manager.

Post Office and Postal Telegraph Office.—Mr. Daniel Till, post master. Letters delivered at 7 a.m. and 1.30 p.m.; despatched 11.40 a.m. and 10 p.m.

Conveyances and Carriers.—To Halesworth, Curtis passes through on Tuesday. To Ipswich, Mayhew, Tuesday and Saturday; Curtis and Meen pass through on Monday. To Saxmundham, Edmonds passes through on Tuesday and Friday. To Stradbroke, Meen passes through on Tuesday. To Woodbridge, Mayhew, daily. Sturgeon, Framlingham to Ipswich, Monday and Thursday, returning the following day. All passing through call at the Chequers.

Posting Establishments.—O. A. Diver, White Hart Hotel; William Foster, Golden Lion Inn.

Surgeons.—Mr. G. Keer, Mr. E. B. Tench, Mr. G. Cochrane.

Working Men's Club and Institute.—Mr. Whitmore, Mr. Binyon, Mr. Barclay Lieut.Col. Lynn, Rev. W. T. Image, Trustees.

Auctioneers.—Messrs. C. H. Read and Son.

Fire Engine.—Mr. A. Nickels, Superintendent.

Agent for the Ipswich Journal, Mr. Minter.

Market day in Thame, Oxfordshire in 1898. The sheep market was held in the long, wide main street.

RUGBY – A DEVELOPING TOWN

In 1831 Rugby had 2,500 inhabitants. This had risen to 7,818 by 1861. Wilson described it in 1876:

> The railway station stands ½ mile N. of the town, is approached by a new street called Albert Street, and is traversed daily by 106 trains. A corn market is held every Tuesday; a butter and poultry market on every Saturday (as well as many fairs).

Look in an atlas and see why Rugby became such an important railway town. Why would a railway station enable the market to expand, especially if cattle, sheep and dairy products were sold?

THAME, OXFORDSHIRE

Fifty years before the photograph was taken Thomas Dugdale, in *England and Wales Delineated*, had written:

> The town consists of principally one long and spacious street, with a very convenient market place in the centre, over which is a town hall. The market is well attended with corn and cattle, and is of great antiquity. The inhabitants are chiefly employed in husbandry [*farming*]; the only manufacture carried on is a little lace, which is made by women and children.

The Village

A Lake District village, c. 1890. Note the stone-built houses and the mounting post to the right.

Not all villages were dependent on agriculture in Victoria's reign. In parts of County Durham and Derbyshire there were, and are, many mining and quarrying villages, whereas in the South West many villages relied on the white clay industry and fishing for their livelihood. As with towns, some villages expanded rapidly, others became suburbs, whilst several continued very much as before.

TWO INDUSTRIAL VILLAGES

Wilson described Washington, County Durham, in 1876:

> The village stands 1 mile NNW of Washington r[ailway] Station. Population in 1851, 1,224; in 1861, 1,829. Houses, 353. There are collieries, blast furnaces, iron works, brick-works and extensive chemical-works. (*Imperial Gazetteer of England and Wales*)

In 1878 James Thorne in his *Environs of London* described Rainham, Essex, where the population in 1871 was 1,122:

> The village extends for some distance along the London road, here a crooked street lined with old fashioned houses and occasional gardens, large coal-yards and wharfs by the brook, which forms a creek navigated by lighters by the bridge . . . . Rainham is the centre and part of an extensive district of market gardens, and a considerable trade is done carrying potatoes and the like by lighters to London and bringing back coal and manure. The neighbour-hood is pleasing, the cottage gardens abound in flowers, and the walks along the uplands N and E afford glimpses of the Thames and the Kentish Hills.

CARSHALTON, SURREY

By contrast, Carshalton, which was three miles west of the expanding town of Croydon and thirteen miles from London by rail, had lost its market and its calico factory but, nevertheless, had grown from 1,775 in 1831 to 3,668 in 1871. Thorne in 1878 described it as:

> a quiet, flourishing village, dependent mainly, perhaps on the resident gentry, but having also manufactories, herb farms, and market gardens. On the [river] Wandle are the paper mills . . . snuff, drug and corn mills; and in summer the fields S. of the Village fill the air for miles with the perfume of lavender, peppermint and other "sweet" herbs.

Can you suggest what the occupations of the villagers would have been? Why did the resident gentry choose to live there?

WILLESDEN

Willesden in Middlesex was only 4½ miles from London. Before the railway came it had a population of 1,413 (in 1831). Forty-seven years later Thorne described it:

> A few years ago Willesden was a quiet, retired, thoroughly rural village, a favourable haunt of the holidaymaker, summer rambler, botanist, and sketcher, who reckoned on the White Horse [Inn] for a substantial country lunch and dinner. Now London has reached its outskirts. The builder has invaded once tranquil meadows, field paths (and fields also) are disappearing, and the lanes for the most part are green no longer, as late as 1861 the population was under 4,000; in 1871 16,000.

What had Willesden become?

Kelly's Post Office Directory of Kent for 1870 *listed the gentry and occupations of the employers of labour in the small village of Chelsfield, Kent (population 1861: 784). Note how many inns there were (those in italics).*

Baugh Rev. Folliott, M.A. [rector]
Crosley Rev. Thomas, B.A. [curate]
Gordon John, Court lodge
Johnson Frederick Godschal
Waring William, J.P. Woodlands
Watson Richard, Pratt's bottom
　　　COMMERCIAL.
Bath Caleb, *Five Bells*
Chatfield Mary (Mrs.), beer retailer
Dunmall William, beer retailer
Fox William Beardsworth, farmer, Lilley's farm

Galloway Thos. *White Hart*, Bo peep
Greaves Sarah (Mrs.), farmer & wheel-wright
Harris Charlotte Ann (Mrs.), farmer
Harris Harry, farmer, Goddington
Haylett Thomas William, blacksmith
Hufford George, tailor
Le Gros Etienne Alexandre, market gardener
Morgan Thomas, farmer
Nightingale Mary Ann (Mrs.), *Bull's Head*

Phillips Ann (Mrs.), farmer, Northsted
Phillips George, farmer & fruit grower, Hewitt's farm
Rock Philip, veterinary surgeon
Smith Richard, beer retailer
Springett Thomas, baker
Staples George, shoe maker
Thompson Henry, grocer & draper
Verrells Priscilla (Mrs.), harness maker
Walton Thomas, farmer & black-smith

THE ISOLATION OF A NORFOLK VILLAGE

Michael Home was born in Norfolk in 1885. In his autobiography, *Winter Harvest: A Norfolk Boyhood* (1967), he describes the village of East Harting where he was born:

> Harting Road Station was even less used; the cheapest fares and excursions to Norwich and Yarmouth were beyond our means. There were plenty of people in the village who had never been outside its boundaries. Even Watton, six miles away was remote. Every Autumn it held an agricultural show, and on that particular morning, a neighbour would hail another with, 'Reckon you'll be goin' to the show?' But that was a joke . . . . Nobody, except perhaps a farmer, ever went to Watton show.

Why do you think the villagers were so isolated even at the end of the century?

Estate Villages

Country villages villages were basically of two kinds, open and closed. The former were not under the control of any one powerful landowner. Labourers rented cottages from tradesmen and small farmers, but if times were hard they faced eviction. Closed or estate villages were under the control of one landowner who rented out the cottages to the workers he employed. Sometimes he was a model employer providing good housing, building the village school and supporting the church.

REPORT ON THE AGRICULTURAL LABOURER, 1893

This Government report was prepared by Arthur Wilson Fox:

> **When comparing the cottages in the two Eastern Counties [Suffolk and Norfolk] with those in the three Northern ones [Northumberland, Cumberland and Lancashire] I should say that the worst and the best are to be found in Norfolk and Suffolk, the worst being chiefly in Open Villages, where impecunious [*short of money*] owners or small and greedy speculators are frequently the landlords.**

Why do you think the two types of villages were so different?

HELMINGHAM, SUFFOLK

The Tollemache family had owned the Suffolk village of Helmingham since the sixteenth century. In the Victorian period John, Baron Tollemache carried out many improvements to the village, building a new school and several semi-detached cottages for the estate workers.

Baron Tollemache hoped that his workers would become self-sufficient by growing their own food. Note the pigsty in the plan. The pig was often the main source of meat in the Victorian countryside.

However, tenants had to agree to certain conditions. In the following contract, what was Baron Tollemache trying to ensure that his workers did?

Cottages in Helmingham, Suffolk, 1983. These are the pair shown in the plan. Note how well-built they are.

CONTRACT BETWEEN JOHN, BARON TOLLEMACHE OF HELMINGHAM AND GEORGE STOCKINGS, 11th OCTOBER, 1883

First   Not to plough any part of the said Allotment-land but to cultivate it with the spade leaving one half wheat, and the other half Peas, Beans, Potatoes and other vegetables.

Second   To attend some place of worship once on each Sabbath Day.

Third   To keep the glass and windows of the said cottage in good repair.

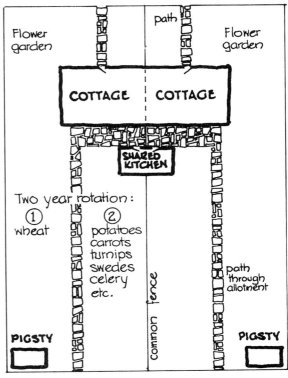

Plan of estate cottages at Helmingham, Suffolk.

ARGUMENTS AGAINST ESTATE VILLAGES

In *Lark Rise to Candleford* Flora Thompson wrote of villagers in an open village in Oxfordshire who felt that paying rent to a landlord who was not their employer gave them greater freedom than people in an estate village:

> **'Stands to reason' they said, 'they're allus got to do just what they be told, or out they goes, neck and crop, bag and baggage.'**

Write down the arguments for and against closed (i.e. estate) villages and try to find out into which category your nearest villages should be placed.

The Cottage

Some Victorian writers had a very romantic view of the homes of the country dwellers, probably having seen them in the warmth of a summer outing. This was the case in John Murray's *Guide to Devonshire*, published in 1851:

> The Devonshire cottage is truly said to be "the sweetest object that the poet, the artist or the lover of the romantic could desire to see." The roof is universally of thatch, and the walls generally of cob, which is a concrete of mud and pebbles, very warm and if kept dry at top and bottom, very durable.

Contrast this with the impression of the Frenchman Hippolyte Taine, who wrote *Notes on England* in 1861. Here he is writing about the Home Counties (those around London):

> Several cottages are very poor, being clay covered with laths and a thatched roof. The rooms are too low and too narrow, the windows too small and the partitions too thin. Think of a large family huddled in winter in two of these rooms with clothes drying, the swaddling clothes of infants, and the chimney roaring . . . .

OVERCROWDING

Flora Thompson described the problem of overcrowding in the poorest homes in her Oxfordshire village in the 1880s and 1890s:

> Some of the cottages had two bedrooms, others only one, in which case it had to be divided by a screen or a curtain to accommodate parents and children. Excepting at holiday times there were no big girls to provide for, as they were all out at service. Still it was often a tight fit, for children swarmed, eight, ten or even more in the families . . . beds and shakedowns [*folding mattresses*] were often so closely packed that the inmates had to climb over one bed to get to another.
>
> In nearly all the cottages there was but one room downstairs, and many of these were poor and bare, with only a table and a few chairs and stools for furniture and a superannuated potato sack thrown down by way of hearth rug. (*Lark Rise to Candleford*)

Why do you think that conditions such as these would have affected health?

A cottage interior in Gresham, Norfolk, in the 1860s. Note the fire, range and objects on the mantelpiece, butter churn to left and plank-top table by the window.

Houses built into red sandstone cliff at Kinver, Staffordshire. Note the girl drawing water from the well.

IN NEED OF REPAIR

Repairs were a constant problem. In *Rural England*, published in 1902, Rider Haggard described some labourers' cottages in Cambridgeshire:

> **No. 1 thatched, built of cracked and ancient stud-work, contained one bedroom, one sitting room and one lean-to scullery. The bedroom in the roof, which was stopped with rags to keep out the rain, was approached by a steep ladder, the woman who led me there crawling upon her hands and knees into the apartment.**

Why would one not have found such a cottage in Helmingham (see pages 10-11)?

THE WATER SUPPLY

Mrs Jekyll, in *Old West Surrey* (1904), described methods of obtaining water in Victorian times:

> **Each cottage, except where they were closely grouped had its well. Down in the valleys where the water is near the surface, it was reached by lowering the pail by a pole with a spring hook at the end, or, if deeper, with a winch and a rope.**

What would be the problem in a long, dry summer or in a very cold winter?

Walk round your nearest village with a 25" map and try to estimate the number of people who lived in the older houses. You may be able to check your guesses against their listings in the Census.

The Country House

Today, many of the larger country houses are open to the public, as the costs of running them have grown. Several of these, such as Woburn and Blenheim, were built in earlier centuries, but during the nineteenth century many more were built. They were often built in various styles of the past, but inside they had all the latest Victorian comforts. Each room had a separate fireplace and each grate had to be cleaned, laid, lit and fed throughout the day. The servants would have been kept busy.

SHRUBLANDS HALL, NORFOLK, 1851

This estate covered twenty square miles and as the information from the Census shows, it was a great employer of labour. It was owned by the Marquis of Hertford.

Indoor		17
Outdoor	Stables	16
	Keepers and night men	16
	Warreners	4
	Parks	10
	Gardeners	40
	Lodge Keepers	3
	Blacksmiths	2
	Carpenters	7
	Painters	3
	Engineers	2
	Home Farm	38
	Brick Kiln	9
	Bricklayers	4
	Wheelwrights	2
Total staff employed		173

You can see that the estate was largely maintained by the servants and that its own bricks were used.

WORKING IN A COUNTRY HOUSE

Servant life must have been long and ardous. Here William Lanceley describes his work as a Hall-boy in 1870:

> My duties, which started at six o'clock A.M., were as follows: first light the servants' hall fire, clean the young ladies' boots, the butler's, housekeeper's, cook's, and ladies-maids', often twenty pairs altogether, trim the lamps, and all this had to be got through by 7.30; then lay up the hall breakfast, get it in, and clear up afterwards. Tea was provided at breakfast for women servants and beer for the men. I was not rated as a man...
>
> My day's work followed on with cleaning knives, house-keeper's room, silver, windows, and mirrors; lay up the servants' hall dinner; get in luncheon; wash up in the pantry; carry up the dinner to the dining-room and when extra people dined, wait at table; lay up the servants' hall supper; clear it over and wash up. This brought bedtime after a day's work of sixteen hours; yet I seldom felt tired as the work was so varied and the food of the best...
>
> (Quoted in J. Burnett, *Useful Toil*)

What do you think were the advantages and disadvantages of working in a country house?

A large income was needed to maintain a large country house. Lady Agnew described how an income of £10,000 per year might be needed. She was writing in the *Cornhill Magazine,* August 1901.

Country property expenses	£2,200
London house, inclusive of rates and taxes, decorations and repairs	£ 800
House books, inclusive of beer and washing and household washing	£1,200
Wages	£ 400
Coal	£ 130
Lighting	£ 70
Liveries (indoor)	£ 70
Butler's book for all postage and letters, parcels, hampers, cabs, etc.	£ 130
Stationery and small bills	£ 150
Wine	£ 200
Entertainment and amusements	£ 350
Upkeep of two houses in linen, general wear and tear, etc.	£ 200
Dress and private expenses (£450 each)	£ 900
Education and children's clothes	£ 500
Stables	£ 600
Small journeys and visits	£ 150
Illness	£ 100
Taxes (income and others)	£ 450
Charities	£ 400
	£9,000

This will leave you with a balance of £1,000 for margin.

Most wealthy people with country estates maintained a house in London and would live there for part of each year. Do you think it is surprising that Lady Agnew suggests donating as much money to charities as was spent on the servants' wages?

Preston Hall, Aylesford, near Maidstone, Kent, c. 1900. This was the recently built home of H.L.C. Brassey J.P. Note the large number of chimneys. The gardens covered some 200 acres.

The hall, Preston Hall. Note the height of the hall and the grand staircase. Can you locate the hall on the other photograph?

The Estate Owner

The very large landowner with an estate of 10,000 acres or more had tremendous power, controlling not only land but also large numbers of people. In some counties such as Northumberland or Rutland half the county was in their hands.

A LARGE LANDOWNER

One such landowner was the Earl of Bathurst who owned much of Cirencester in Gloucestershire and the surrounding countryside. His power was described by Richard Jefferies in *Hodge and his Master,* published in 1880:

> A peer only at Westminster, here he is a prince, whose dominions are almost co-extensive with the horizon; and this, the capital city, is for the most part his.
>   Far away stretches that little Kingdom, with its minor towns and villages, hamlets and farms. Broad green meadows, where the cattle graze beside the stream and in the plains; rolling uplands, ploughed and sown, where the barley flourishes; high hills and shadowy woods; grey church towers, new glaring schools; quiet wayside inns, and ancient farmhouses tenanted for generations by the same families.

This is part of the page from George Warde Norman's Labour Book. How many different jobs can you identify? Roughly how much a day were they paid? This and similar materials will be found in your local library or record office. This one comes from the Kent Record Office. Don't be put off by the handwriting. Remember, it is a contemporary, working document.

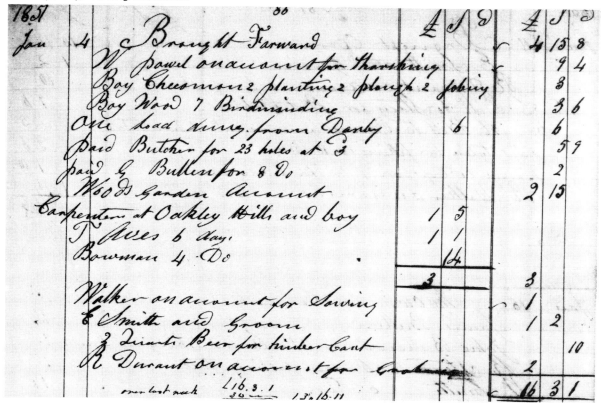

A LOCAL LANDOWNER

Very few landowners owned as much land as the Earl of Bathurst. George Warde Norman was one of the four leading landowners in Bromley, Kent, owning roughly 700 acres. He was an important local figure and magistrate. In his Memoir he described how he improved his home.
(Note: "do" = ditto; "underpinning" = foundations.)

Repairs and additions 1858-1861

Geo. Gill. New Buildings	£2,946.12.11
East Front. Underpinning and Portico.	598. 0. 6
Do. End of Drawing Room Do.	
Do. & West end of Dining Room Do. & West Porch rebuilt.	657.10. 6
School Room underpinning and Library Area and Servants' Hall &c.	538.18.11
Sundries House (various items on the house)	113.18. 5
Stables	199.12. 4
J. Nettlfold. Upholsterer	180.16. 2
Deane & Co. Grates	30.15. 0
Lapworth. Carpets	103. 2.10
Purdie & Co. Painters & Decorators	195.13. 0
Edwards. Chimney Piece. Drawing Room	28.12. 0
Waring & Blake	269.19. 6
Gill. Fives Court	161. 5. 4
William Bailey & Son. Kitchen Range	75. 6. 4
Bromley Gas. Co.	130. 6. 9
Servants' Hall & underpinning School Room	538.18.11
Decoration of Dining Room &c.	140. 2. 0
	£6,909.11. 5

The estate servants at Netley Hall, Shropshire, c. 1880. There are two gamekeepers, three gardeners, a groom, a coachman and a carpenter. Can you identify each of them?

This was the exact expense so far as I can make it out, without going over all my account again, but I think it probable, that I have omitted some items.

In fact, the old man listed one item twice. Which was this?

In addition, George Warde Norman ran a working farm on his estate. Look at the extract from his Labour Book – an account book listing payments to those employed and often the work they did.

The Village Church

Each parish had its Anglican church and the vicar was second in importance in the village only to the landowner.

THE VICAR OF ORPINGTON, 1851

The Census of 1851 gives us the following detail. The vicar seems to have been recently widowed and the nurse would have looked after the children. The footman would have acted also as coachman and probably slept above the stables. There is no housekeeper. Who do you think was in charge of the servants?

Street, Place, Road, House, Etc.	Name and Surname	Relationship to Head of Family	Condition M(arried) U(nmarried) W(idower)	Age	Rank, Profession or Occupation	Where Born
Church Hill Vicarage	William Falconer	Head	W	48	Vicar of Orp. with St. Mary Cray	Cumberland
	Jane E. ,,	Daughter	U	7	Vicar's Daughter	Sussex
	Joanna S. ,,	,,	U	5	,,	,,
	Joanna Simmons	Aunt	U	66	Vicar's Aunt	Hastingleigh
	Ann Perry	Servant	U	52	Nurse	Essex
	Elizabeth Taylor	,,	U	32	Cook	Riverhead
	Ann Marchant	,,	U	28	Housemaid	Glos.
	James Waghorne	,,	U	24	Footman	Sevenoaks
	Catherine Cooke	,,	U	21	Housemaid	Middx.

GOING TO CHURCH, c. 1870

In some villages going to church was not a matter of choice, as R.L. Gales recalled in *The Vanished Country Folk,* published in 1914.

"Bless the squire and his relatives
And keep us in our proper stations."
– that was the way of it. The labourers and their families all came to church – they would have got the sack if they hadn't. The big farmers had a man at the Church door to tell them off one by one as they came in. Any absentee would be reported on Monday morning and if a satisfactory explanation was not forthcoming he would have to go. The Squire's party came first for Communion .... They knelt in the middle of the altar-rails and received the bread and the wine. After that came the rest of the congregation, first the farmers, then the tradesmen, and so on, and last the labourers.

Why did the farmer have such power over the labourer?

CHURCH MUSIC

Today most churches have an organ. This was not always so. Mrs A.C. Day's book *Glimpses of Rural Sussex* includes an interview in the 1920s with Henry Smith of Hadlow Green, Sussex, who described his church in 1850:

> **There were no organs in churches or chapels in the country, the musical portion of the service being led by a band containing a variety of instruments. At Hadlow Down Church, Jack Wren of Blackboys played the bass viol, his son the bassoon, and Walter Bean the clarionet.**

The musicians often played in the gallery. Many of these have now been taken down, but see if you can find one still remaining.

Michael Home mentions another difference in his remote Norfolk village:

> **Many of the older ones could neither read nor write, and in the chapel the first verse of a hymn would be read aloud so that everyone could identify it.**
> (*Winter Harvest*, 1967)

A Shropshire church in the 1860s. Can you identify the worker?

IN WINTER

Many rural churches were unheated in the winter, as this extract from the diary of a vicar, R.F. Kilvert, shows:

> **Preached at Clyro in the morning . . . . Very few people in Church, the weather fearful, violent deadly E. wind and the hardest frost we have had yet. Went to Bettws in the afternoon wrapped in two waistcoats, two coats, a muffler and a mackintosh, and was not at all too warm . . . . When I got to the Chapel my beard moustaches and whiskers were so stiff with ice that I could hardly open my mouth and my beard was frozen on to my mackintosh. There was a large Christening party from Llywyn Gwilym. The baby was baptised in ice which was broken and swimming about in the Font.**

Working on the Land

Farm labourers who lived in with a farmer, or were employed on an estate, had the greater security. For the majority, work was seasonal. In the winter there may have been little to do, whilst in the summer many extra hands would be needed. Frequently, the labourer had to walk several miles each day to and from work. This often happened if the village was an open one and there were more workers than available jobs.

FARMING TASKS

Even after the introduction of machinery, most of the work was still done by horses and men. Some of the tasks were unskilled, like picking stones, but many required a lot of skill – far more than the word "labourer" implies.

These are some of the activities listed in George Warde Norman's labour book for the year 1851:

> planting, thrashing [*threshing*], birdminding, dung loading and carrying, digging holes, grubbing, ratcatching, filling holes, ditching, clearing oats, hedging, spreading dung, picking stones, cutting bushes, hay binding, fencing, cutting drains, planting potatoes, ploughing.

Which of these jobs were (a) skilled, (b) probably done by women and children?

CHARLES LAST – PLOUGHMAN

Ploughmen were often the best-paid workers because they were the most skilled. They were judged by their ability to plough a straight furrow and drill evenly. George Ewart Evans in *Where Beards Wag All* recorded an interview with Charles Last, born in Suffolk in 1878, who remembered the turn of the century:

An old lady carrying peat, taken c. 1900 in Shropshire. Note her laced boots and the wicker panier. What would the peat have been used for?

After I'd been there [Mr. Hunt's farm, Needham Market] some years I was out a-ploughing one morning and Mr. Hunt, the farmer himself, was there. After a while another farmer came by and come into the field; and as he see me a-going round he say: "You got one good ploughman at least", and when I turned round at the headlings [*headlands*] he say to me:

> "You been at this game some while, Mister."
> "More'n three weeks!"
> "I dessay."
> "I'll tell you what: I've been at this game long enough to git twelve copper kittles."

How do you think he got 12 copper kettles?

A SUSSEX FARMHOUSE SERVANT IN 1855

Mrs Wren was 90 when she was interviewed by Mrs Day in *Glimpses of Rural Life in Sussex* (1927). In 1855 she earned 3/9d per week.

> Three men were boarded in the farmhouse. There were 10 cows for the men to milk. Milking did not come into my work, but they taught me how to do it. Except a couple of hours' during the afternoon I worked from five in the morning till nearly 10 at night. You see there were six people in the house, Master, Missus, three men and myself. We baked, brewed, churned, made up 50-70 pounds of butter a week, besides doing all the washing, cooking and cleaning that was needed. Then I had the little chickens and ducklings to mind till they were big enough to sell to the higgler [*trader*].

In addition to other farm products such as fruit and vegetables, which foods would have had to be bought?

An old man at Water Orton, Warwickshire, 1893. Is this how James Rogers would have dressed?

A FARM LABOURER'S DRESS IN 1850

Today the dress of the Victorian farm worker would look rather strange, but it had to be serviceable and was used throughout the year. James Rogers of Rotherfield, Sussex, was interviewed by Alice Catherine Day in 1927 for her book *Glimpses of Rural Life in Sussex*.

> Would you like to see me in my round smock frock? Well, here it is. I will put it on, and also my round smock hat. Of course, we always wore corduroy trousers like these I have on. In summer we tied them under the knees in order to shorten them, and in winter we wore long leather gaiters, reaching half-way up our thighs.

THE TURF DIGGER

Turf was dug from the Fens. Sybil Marshall in *Fenland Chronicle* (1967) gives her father's account of the problems faced in this remote corner of England in late Victorian times:

> For the first few weeks of the season the diggers would suffer agony with their hands. The bottom hand, that is, the hand nearer the blade of the tool, got blisters from the constant friction, often as round as a halfpenny. We used to deal with these by threading a needle with wool, and drawing it through the blister, cutting the ends off, and leaving the wool to drain the blister dry.

What do you think the turf would have been used for?

Working in the Woods

Woodland played a major part in the building, brewing, furniture, shipping and carriage industries. Wood sawyers and wood brokers were found in the wooded parts of practically every parish, even those fairly near London.

AN ORPINGTON SAWYER IN 1851

Orpington, Kent, is 15 miles from London, and is today a suburb.

Street, Place, Road, House, Etc.	Name and Surname	Relationship to Head of Family	Condition M(arried) U(nmarried) W(idower)	Age	Rank, Profession or Occupation	Where Born
Reynolds Smith	William Ingarfill	Head	M	66	Sawyer	Surrey
	Jane „	Wife	M	49	Sawyer's Wife	Edenbridge
	Edward „	Son	U	22	Sawyer	St. Pauls Cray
	George „	Son	U	17	Paper Finisher	Orpington
	Michael „	Son	U	19	Sawyer	Orpington

THE WOODMEN

In 1908 G.W. Smith of Bromley, Kent, wrote down his recollections of the 1870s:

Our district being well-wooded, during winter, most of the old people worked in connection with the woods. As a youngster, I can remember the charcoal burners at work in Crofton Woods, stacking the wood and covering it with earth, [and] all the Wattle and daub makers. Then the hop pole shavers ... pale cleavers and sawyers, all worked in the woods. Another trade has quite disappeared, the spile or vent pegs [*plugs for beer barrels*] were made and sent to the London breweries when I was a child. They were mostly made from clean grown hazel rods but it has given way to machine made spiles.

Note how machines have taken over work done in the home by hand.

BARK STRIPPERS AT WORK

In this extract from Thomas Hardy's *The Woodlanders* (1887), the author describes bark strippers at work in south west England. Note that, although this is from a novel, it is an accurate description. Compare the top photograph with Hardy's description.

The barking season had just commenced, and what he had heard was the tear of the ripping-tool as it ploughed its way along the sticky parting between the trunk and the rind ....

Each tree doomed to the flaying process was first attacked by Upjohn. With a small bill-hook he carefully freed the collar of the tree from twigs and patches of moss which encrusted it to a height of a foot or two above the ground .... After this it was barked in its erect position as high as a man could reach ....

These men are working in Crofton Woods, near Bromley, Kent, c. 1870. Why was it more efficient for them to work as a team? Note the tools they are using.

Brusher Mills, New Forest snake catcher, alongside the Charcoal Burner's hut where he lived. He caught adders and other snakes, for which he received 1/– each.

As soon as it had fallen the barkers attacked it like locusts, and in a short time not a particle of rind was left on the trunk and larger limbs. Marty South was adept at peeling the upper parts; and there she stood encaged amid the mass of twigs and buds like a great bird, running her ripping-tool into the smallest branches . . . .

THE CHARCOAL BURNER

Charcoal was used mainly in the manufacture of iron. The industry flourished in the wooded areas of the country up to the mid-eighteenth century. However, the industry continued throughout the nineteenth century and the workers moved from site to site, building temporary huts in the clearings they had made. The Weald and Downland Museum has reconstructed a charcoal burner's site (see Places to Visit, page 46).

Once the charcoal had been produced, it was then bagged and transported to the nearest road or station. Arthur Cooke in *The Forest of Dean*, published in 1912:

When once the charcoal is bagged the Charcoal burners' work is done. With the carrying of half hundred weight bags up the steep and slippery hillside to the nearest cart track or with the struggles of the woodland wagon team in miry and deep-rutted ways, he has no concern. But he recalls the fact that, many years ago and five and twenty miles from where we stand, there were men who maintained large teams of donkeys . . . twenty and thirty in a team; and that the patient little beasts would daily travel some twelve miles or more, threading the woodland paths between the charcoal burners and the nearest railway station, each with a bag of charcoal on its back.

Try to find out what the charcoal and bark would have been used for.

Rural Gangs

Gangs of women and children were often employed on farms to do hard, time-consuming jobs, or at a particular time, such as potato picking, when extra labour was needed. The gangs usually worked for an individual who would receive a lump sum from the farmer, which he would divide among the gang after taking his own profit.

IRISH GANGS IN 1862

Some of the organized gangs would travel the country in the summer, seeking work. A.J. Munby, a London solicitor, met an Irish gang in Yorkshire, as he recorded in his diary for October 1862:

> **I returned to York by Garrow Hill and overtook a dozen Irishwomen returning from field work near Heslington. They had been tatergathering. Wages 1/– a day for other labour, but 1/3d. for this, because it's hard: we have to be on our knees in the furrows all day long sometimes; scarce ever a chance to straighten one's back. After taters [*potatoes*] comes turnip pulling, and then we are idle all winter and live on what we earned in the Summer.**

CHILD GANGS

The gangs which caused the most concern were those which included young children, many of whom were girls. In *I Walked by Night, by the King of the Norfolk Poachers* (an anonymous autobiography of a Victorian poacher), the author described the situation in Norfolk in about 1860:

> **The children was sent out at an early age into the fields to work, scaren crows and such like jobs. I can well remember wen lots of poor Children had to go to work in the spring of the year, picken foule grass ... from eight in the morning till five in the afternoon, some with scarse any boots on there feet. The Master would send a man to keep them at work, and he would stand in the field with a stick or whip to keep them at it. Wen they had done the day's work they would get the sum of three pence.**

This was written some years afterwards. Compare it with the evidence presented on these pages and list the worst aspects of child gangs.

ROYAL COMMISSION EVIDENCE

Royal Commissions were established to investigate particular problems. Evidence was collected throughout the country by investigators who interviewed all the people concerned. The Sixth Report of the Commissioners of the Children's Employment Commission (1862) said:

3. The system of "organized" labour known by the name of "agricultural gangs" exists, as far as we have been able to ascertain, almost exclusively in the following counties:–

Lincolnshire, Huntingdonshire, Cambridgeshire, Norfolk, Suffolk, Nottinghamshire.

There are a few instance of the employment of these gangs in three other neighbouring counties...namely, in the counties of Northampton, Bedford, and Rutland.

4. They are not found over the whole of any of these counties, but are distributed irregularly through various parts of them, in obedience to local circumstances.

5. An organized agricultural gang consists of–
   1. The gang master.
   2. A number of
      (a) Women.
      (b) Young persons of both sexes. It will be convenient, in designating "young persons," to adopt the definition of the Factory Acts, namely, those between 13 and 18.
      (c) Children of both sexes from the age of 6 to 13.

6. The "organized gang,"– the subject of the present inquiry, – is called in some districts the "public gang," in others the "common gang;" in some places it is called the "jobbing gang;" elsewhere the "travelling gang." We purpose following in this Report the term "public gang," as perhaps the most usual and the most distinctive.

7. The numbers in each public gang are from 10 or 12 to 20, 30, and 40; very rarely above 40. But the most common, because the most manageable number, is about 20.

Look at a map and locate the counties which the Inspectors studied.

AFTER THE GANGS ACT

Finally, in 1867 a Gangs Act was passed which required the licensing of gangs and forbad the use of child labour. The spread of schooling helped, but the problem was still there in 1890. The following log was written by the Headmaster of Helmingham School:

> 1890 April. Farmers have a great wish to employ children at stone picking, but so far I have prevented many, except those above the Fourth standard, from joining a gang.

WILLIAM BENSLEY OF NORFOLK

In 1893 a Report was presented to Parliament on the Depressed State of Farming. The Royal Commission had interviewed many workers. William Bensley gave his evidence in August 1892:

> I am 21 years of age. I began work with the gangs after I left school at thirteen years of age, and worked for three years.
>
> In Swaffham there are three gangs, one a woman's gang, which consists of girls and some married women, about 20 in all.
>
> There are two boys' gangs about 25 in each. When I first joined the gang I earned 8d. a day. I daresay the farmer paid the gang master 1/– a day for my work. When I was 16 I earned 10d. a day. We began work in the summer at 8 AM and left off at 5 PM with an hour for dinner between 12 and one. In the winter we worked from 8 AM to 3 PM and half an hour to three quarters off for dinner. When working with a gang we would work much harder than at day work.

How much did he earn in a six-day week in summer, at age 16, and how many hours would he have had to put in?

Children at Work

THE CYCLE OF CHILDREN'S WORK IN NORFOLK, ESSEX, SUSSEX AND GLOUCESTERSHIRE

The following list is drawn from Mr Frazer's (one of the Government Inspectors) report to the Agricultural Employment Commission of 1867-69.

January	Hop pole shaving and other coppice work in woodland counties.
February	Twitching, stone pick, bean and pea setting.
March	Potato setting, bird scaring, cleaning land for spring corn.
April	Bird scaring, weeding corn, setting potatoes.
May	Bird scaring, weeding corn, clearing land for turnips.
June	Haymaking, turnip singling.
July	Turnip singling, pea picking, cutting thistles, scaring birds from ripening corn.
August	Corn harvesting, gleaning.
September	Hop harvest, tending sheep or pigs on the stubble.

Child labour was very common in the Victorian period and from an early age a child was used to going out into the fields to help his parents. At harvest time the whole family would be employed, but throughout the year there were many jobs that children could do. The majority of children did not work in gangs.

October	Potato and fruit gathering, twitching, dropping wheat.
November	Bird scaring from new sown wheat and beans, acorning.
December	Stone picking, spreading cow droppings, in Norfolk scaring birds from corn stacks; in Essex helping their fathers to make surface drains; in woodland districts, coppice work; topping and tailing turnips and clearing roots for cattle.

Try to draw up a similar table for either a grazing county or the one in which you live

Staffordshire farm workers. Which of the group do you think would still be at school nowadays?

ALFRED IRESON'S FIRST JOB

Alfred Ireson was born in 1856. In his authobiography written in 1929 he describes his first job in Northamptonshire in the late 1860s:

> **My first job was on a farm. My wages were 1/6d. a week. My work was to scare crows from the newly growing corn. A pair of clappers was provided. When the crows came I had to send them off to other fields to feed. I had to be up with the crows, and did not go home until the last had gone to bed – 14 or 15 hours a day. Then my wages were advanced to 2/6d. a week, but for the additional 1/–, about a dozen pigs were put under my care.** (Quoted in J. Burnett, *Destiny Obscure*)

How does his wage compare with that of William Bensley on page 25?

LEADING HORSES

Some of the jobs could be both dangerous and tiring. Arthur Randell describes his work at the turn of the century in *Sixty Years a Fenman,* published in 1966. He began work at the age of eight, at 6 a.m.

> **I was taken to a field of Wheat where a six sailed reaping machine, with four horses attached, was waiting .... I was to ride the offside front horse, keeping it close to the standing corn, then pull out on reaching the corner and then swing back .... The horses were changed at 10, 2 and 6 o'clock; there was no dinner break .... I spent three weeks riding the reaping horse, then I was switched over to leading the horse and shouting "Hold tight".**

COPPER HOLE JACK

In *I Walked By Night, By the King of the Norfolk Poachers,* the anonymous author describes the first job he had on leaving school in 1873 at the age of 13:

> **The first Job I had was what was called Copper Hole Jack, I had to light the fires, help the servants and make myself generally useful all round. Now a lad like that would be called a House Boy, and Verry Properly be put in uniform. The people that I went to work for were Gentleman Farmers. I had to be at work at 6AM till 6PM and Sundays much the same owers.**

Poaching was eventually to lead him into trouble and prison, as the next extract tells.

A CHILD POACHER

> **After a littel I got a Job as Page Boy to a Shepperd. It was more to my liken there – I could carry on the game [poaching] to my hart's content. Of course the Shepperd was as bad as I was, no one ever guessed our Job.**

After pheasants he turned to rabbits, but was eventually caught by a Policeman and a Gamekeeper. He was taken to Norwich Prison after being sentenced to one month's hard labour.

> **I was taken to Norwich by train, handcuffed to a Policeman. Wen I got to Norwich I was led through the streets the same way like a real dangerous fellow. There were no cabs then for prisoners, and evry one could have a good stare at me as I went by ... at last we arrived at the Castle Entrance. A door swung open and a Turnkey led us inside. I shall never forget what I felt when I first saw that gloomy Place and I was just fit to cry, but held back my tears somehow.**

Hops and Hop Picking

PREPARING THE POLES

Hops require a lot of labour at particular times. Poles have to be prepared, placed in position and the bines intertwined. The labour book of the Peel Estate in Kent contains the following examples:

April 26th, 1850
Mrs. Wenham and others –
    shaving 2000 12 foot poles   10/–d.
April 11th, 1851
Kitty Tree – shaving 500 14 foot
    poles   3/4d.

Why do you think it was necessary to shave the poles?

Name	Task	Days	Pay
Mrs. Hyde	laddertying	5 days	5 – 0
Mrs. Edmonds	,,	5 ,,	5 – 0
Mrs. Kitchenham	,,	5 ,,	5 – 0
Mrs. Reader	,,	5 ,,	5 – 0
Mrs. Comber	,,	3½ ,,	3 – 6
Mrs. Ashby	,,	3 ,,	3 – 0

Note the two different methods of payment, by the day or by the job. Which would you prefer?

TYING THE BINES

Bines are the hop plants and they would be intertwined to the poles. *The Agricultural Gazette* of 10 May 1874 described the process:

Tying hops is very pleasant work for women when the weather is good ... [it] requires dexterity in fastening the rushes around the tender heads of the bines, not too tight to stop their progress upwards, nor too loose to allow them to slip back again ...

The nineteenth century was the golden age of hop growing and the greatest acreage devoted to it was reached in 1878. The most important hop county was Kent, though hops were grown in the majority of the English counties.

A print showing a family at work picking hops. Note the wicker baskets and the hop poles.

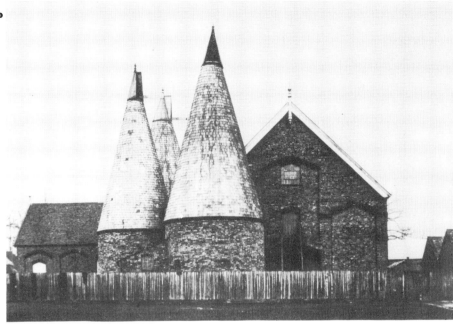

Oast houses on the Palace Estate, Bromley, 1928. The estate prided itself on having the first hops to reach the London market.

A Victorian oast house.

HOP FIELDS IN KENT

William Howitt in *Visits to Remarkable Places*, published in 1840, described the hop fields around Penshurst, Kent, in late September:

> Green fields and rustic cottages interspersed among woods; and the picturesque hop-grounds on the steep slopes and the hollows of the hills, now in their full glory; and all the rural population out and busy in gathering the hops . . .
>
> The whole road as I came from town [Tonbridge] was thronged with huge wagons of pockets of new hops piled nearly as high as the houses they passed . . . and here, at almost every farm house and group of cottages, you perceived the rich aromic odour of hops, and saw the smoke issuing from the cowls of the drying kilns.

From this description, jot down your impressions of what life must have been like for the people at work in the hop areas of Kent. Then compare what you

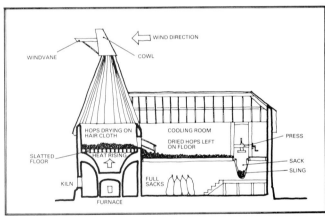

have written with the following by the Reverend J.J. Kendon who visited the Wealden village of Goudhurst in the 1860s. Try to decide why the impressions are so different.

> They sleep . . . almost like the cattle in the fields. To mingle with these poor creatures, to see their habits and hear their language, to witness the awful length to which they go makes it seem almost impossible that we can be living . . . in the nineteenth century.

Harvest Time

PREPARATIONS

In *I Walked by Night,* we have an account of the arrangements which an individual Norfolk farmer made with his own workers for extra work;

> Harvest was a great event in them days, the great time of the whole year. The Farmer would call his men together wen he thought the corn was ripe for cutten, and tell them they would start harvest on a certain day. He also told them the price that he would pay them for it and they had no option but to agree.

Why do you think the men could not challenge the payment that was offered?

LONG HOURS AND HARD WORK

Mrs Hurst, interviewed by Alice Catherine Day in *Glimpses of Rural Life in Sussex* (1927), described how she took her children harvesting in 1875.

> After an early breakfast I used to start with my children for one of the Hall fields, carrying our dinner with us, also sometimes a kettle in order to make some hot tea. Even the toddlers could

Harvest was a time when extra help was needed. It was also an opportunity for families to earn extra money to see them through the winter. Often, whole families would be involved.

> help by twisting the straw into bands and helping me tie the sheaves. The children enjoyed being out of doors. But cutting and binding the sheaves was not the end of our day's works, we still had to make the shocks. Many is the time that my husband came round to us when his own day's work was done, and we worked together setting up the shocks by moonlight.

Richard Jefferies in *The Field and Hedgerow,* published in 1889, describes how hard the work was on the hands:

> Next day the village sent forth the army with their crooked weapons to cut and slay . . . your skins and mine could not have stood the scratching of the straw, which is stiff and sharp, and the burning of the sun, which blisters like a red hot iron. No one could stand the harvest field as a reaper except he had been born [to it].

HARVEST CELEBRATIONS

In *I Walked by Night,* we have a description of the scene in Norfolk in the 1860s when the crops were finally gathered in:

> **The farmer would come out and pay the men, give them plenty of beer, and of cors make a bit of a speach. Then he would give the Harvest supper, and they would have a wonderful spread, with a good fat sheep, or Beef, and more Beer. Some times the supper was held in the Farmers barn and some times at a Public [house].**

During the celebrations speeches would be made and songs would be sung.

> ### The Master's Good Health
> **Here's a health unto our Master, the founder of the Feast,**
> **I wish with all my heart and soul in Heaven he may find rest.**
> **I hope all things may prosper, that ever he takes in hand,**
> **For we are all his servants, and all at his command.**
> **Drink, boys, drink, and see you do not spill,**
> **For if you do, you must drink two, it is your Master's will.**

Coles Child of Bromley, Kent, gave his Harvest Home in the barn of Palace Farm (see the photograph on page 29) in September 1863. The *Bromley Record* reported that one hundred workers and their wives attended, and the toast to the Lord and his son and heir was given by one of the workers. In it he said:

> **his interest was ours and ours was his, that he found the capital and brain to direct, we the bone and sinew to do the same.**

What impression do you get from the last two extracts of the attitude of the worker to his employer?

THE EXTRA MONEY IS SPENT

Walter Rose, in *Good Neighbours,* published in 1942, recalled Haddenham, Bucks, where:

> **Everyone looked to harvest earnings for the extra money for boots for the family. And the bootmaker knew this and worked to it; the many pairs he made in advance (on that understanding) were a very important part of his livelihood. The village feast fell at a lucky time for all concerned – just on the edge of winter, when back money, due on harvest earnings, had to be paid.**

Look back at these extracts and decide why, although harvest time was such hard work, it was also important and enjoyable.

◁ *A sail reaper in Oxfordshire, c. 1900. When the tray was full, the following boy would pull off the load and it would be bound and placed into stooks.*

Country Crafts

Village craftsmen such as wheelwrights, blacksmiths, carpenters, saddlers and coopers not only made tools and household objects but also carried out major repairs. Even after the coming of the railway they continued to play a vital role.

A wheelwright's yard in Buckinghamshire. What might the large wheels have been used on?

THE BLACKSMITH

Charles Cooper was born in Ashdon, near Saffron Walden, Essex. In Ketteridge and Mays' *Five Miles from Bunkum* (1972) they describe his work around the beginning of the twentieth century:

> **Farm workers came with problems, for most of the labourers had to find their own tools. They asked for left handed scythes, wide or narrower hoe blades to chop out weeds from wide or narrow drillings; men with big arms would demand scythe blades, and gamekeepers and poachers asked for long bladed curved spades to dig out rabbits and ferrets. He sharpened bill-books, scythes, sickles, axes and every type of edged tool, often replacing the broken . . . [pieces]. He made pitchforks and four-tined plough studs, cutters, shears, drills and harrows; sometimes renewing the entire set of teeth on worn out harrows.**

Find out what the various agricultural instruments were used for. Which domestic ones might he have made?

THE WHEELWRIGHT

The wheelwright was another skilled craftsman. George Ewart Evans interviewed Percy Wilson (born 1884) of Witnesham, Suffolk. He began his apprenticeship at 15.

> **When I was an apprentice we used to go out during the winter to cut down the trees we wanted. We put them on a timber jim – a large wheeled trolley – and carted them home into the yard.**
> **Then the trunk would be cut in the saw pit.**
> **When the tree had been marked out the boy – the bottom sawyer – got into**

the pit; the Wheelwright was the top sawyer and was in charge of the work. You had no job to keep warm even in the frostiest weather; you'd have to have your coat off. Each sawyer had to see that he kept to the line while he was sawing; and it was pity help the boy if he didn't keep to the line down in the pit though sometimes he could hardly see it. (From George Ewart Evans, *Where Beards Wag All,* 1970)

Why was the bottom sawyer's job so unpleasant and difficult?

STRAW PLAITING

Straw plaiting was practised in many Bedfordshire villages and in some there were straw plaiting schools. These were really workshops where young children learnt the trade. In 1871 a Government Inspector of Factories visited Bedfordshire:

> **On the opposite side of Dunstable I visited the Villages of Selsworth, Stanbride, and Eggington; there is no school in any of these villages, but I visited seven straw-plaiting schools and found 85 children under 13 working in them. I saw at least 20 to 30 others in the lanes and at the doors of cottages.**

Why was the Inspector concerned at what he found?

NUMBERS EMPLOYED IN COUNTRY CRAFTS (1861 – 1901)

Occupational Group	1861	1881	1901
1. Farriers and veterinary surgeons	6,800	7,510	2,940
2. Blacksmiths	108,170	112,520	137,070
3. Saddlers and Whip Harnessmakers	19,410	28,870	30,680
4. Straw manufacturers, including bonnets	48,040	30,980	16,280
5. Thatchers	5,360	3,720	Not known
6. Basketmakers – all cane, rush, willow crafts	8,950	11,540	11,520
7. Coopers	17,820	18,700	15,780
8. Wheelwrights	30,070	28,730	28,920
9. Millwrights	8,220	6,940	5,290
10. Carpenters, joiners	177,970	235,230	270,710
11. Clog, shoe, boots and patten makers	255,580	224,100	251,140

(Based on the Census)

Which of the above occupations were largely concerned with wood? Which showed the greatest increase and which the greatest fall? Note the number of trades which are present-day surnames.

Inns and Fairs

The local inn and the fair provided the main entertainment for country people. Villages and towns which retained their markets and fairs throughout the nineteenth century remained important centres for the surrounding countryside. Many fairs were lost with the coming of the railway or the extension of the town into the countryside. Those that remained were not only important for the farmer but also gave pleasure to the country people.

Skittles at the Queen and Castle Inn, Kenilworth, Warwickshire in 1901. Note the earth floor and the "quart" jugs used for drinking. Why do you think the inn is so-named?

FEW AMUSEMENTS

J.S. Fletcher in *Recollections of a Yorkshire Village* (1910) described life in Darrington in the 1870s:

> **Their amusements were few .... The labourer's life ... was work and rest, of honest, healthy, wholehearted play he had none ... his only amusements were the drinking of a pint of beer at the inn and the ... village feast, which was celebrated once a year. Nothing was known of bank holidays; even on Good Friday and Christmas Day the labourer had to do certain work about the farm.**

Not much beer could be afforded. Why, then, did the inn mean so much to the village labourer?

A HIRING FAIR

Servants and labourers who wanted a living-in job with a farmer went to annual hiring fairs to find an employer. In *Far from the Madding Crowd* (1874-76), Thomas Hardy describes one such fair in south west England:

> **At one end of the street stood two to three hundred blithe and hearty labourers waiting upon chance – ... carters and waggoners were distinguished by having a piece of whip-cord twisted round their hats; thatchers wore a fragment of woven straw; shepherds had their sheep-crooks in their hands; and thus the situation required was known to the hirers at a glance ... with his fastening money [a small sum paid by the employer to seal the contract] the labourer would set off to sample the fun of the fair or to buy presents, clothes, food or drink – or ballads. They were sold in hundreds and thousands by itinerant-vendors at fairs and markets.**

Sometimes, warnings were given in song, as in this verse from Horley, in Surrey, c. 1850:

> Come all you jolly ploughing boys
> that whistle through the fair
> Beware of going to Sawyer who lives
> near Horley here,
> For he's the worst master
> that we ever saw
> We ploughing boys have taken an oath
> We won't go there any more.

In this next song, why do you think the labourer is urged to hold out for £10 a year before he is hired?

> So to the hirings we have come, all for to
> look for places,
> If with the master you agree and he will
> give you good wages
> The master that a servant wants will
> now stand in a wonder;
> You must ask ten pounds a year and
> none of you go under.
> It's you that must do all the work and
> what do they require
> So now stand up for wages, lads, before
> that you do hire.

£10 a year seems to have been fairly common. Would you have preferred to be a labourer employed by the day for 2/– or 3/–, or one living in with the farmer for 3/– to 4/– a week?

CHISLEHURST FAIR

George Jessup in *Cheery and Chatty Recollections of Bromley and Neighbourhood in the Past 75 years*, written in 1917, describes the rough and brutal sports enjoyed by the local people.

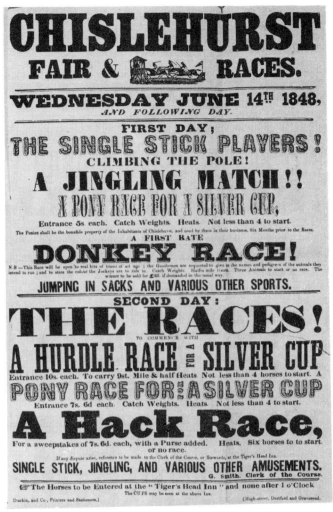

A poster advertising Chislehurst Fair in 1848. The races probably took place on the adjoining Common.

> In a grassy hollow I saw single stick between men stripped to the waist who battered each other till the blood was drawn. Then came several men blindfolded and a man carrying a bell, which he would ring and dodge the blindnesses [the blindfolded men] who darted from the spot where the bell sounds.

Look at the Chislehurst poster and identify the "sports" described in the extract. The grassy hollow had been the village cockpit until that sport had been banned by Act of Parliament.

Upper-Class Leisure

Eva Knatchbull Hugesson was 13 years old in 1874 and lived at Smeeth in East Kent. Her diary is now in the Kent Record Office in Maidstone. This is the entry for 12-15 April, 1874. Make a list of her various leisure activities and interests. How can you tell that she came from a rich family?

By the end of the century there were many people who looked down on the simple pleasures of the ordinary man. Drink was regarded as leading to poverty, whilst fairs were often noisy, brutal and boisterous affairs. Cock fighting and bull baiting were banned early in the century, and several of the fairs were eventually stopped.

(16)

April 12th Sunday. Quite "Wet". We did not go out all day. Papa & Todd went to church in the morning. We all had service in the hall. In the afternoon Mama read to us the "Christian Martyrs".

13th Monday. Showery. We did not go out in the morning. Papa Ned Todd & Cecil played fives, Kate marks I drew, wrote my diary, painted etc. — In the afternoon we all went to Hatch to see the steeple chases. Katie & I were on the two little ponies. Aunt Mary & Cousin Beatrice were there. Towards the end they were leading one of the horses away, when Cousin Wyndham got too near & it kicked him badly on the

leg. He nearly fainted. Blundell ran & got him brandy & he managed to up to the house. The doctor say he ought to lay up for fa fortnight, but he won't hear of it.

14th Tuesday. — Showery. Ned went to Dover agai we went to see him off. We played croquet when came back. Kate & I went the little ponies to ask af C. Wyndham. He is getting very well: they say he broken a muscle: then we had a nice ridge all over Park.

15th Wednesday. Showery. We three played about the haystack, Katie tol us a good story, about

THE VILLAGERS' AMUSEMENTS
UNDER ATTACK

Alfred Williams in *Villages of the White Horse* (in Berkshire) (1913) described the reactions of the upper classes to the fairs and other entertainments enjoyed by the country people:

> The village fair and club festivals were condemned because simple people assembled together to indulge in simple amusements. The sight of so many poor foolish peasant folk thronging the streets; the Henries, and Thomases, the Emmas and Mary Anns, laughing immoderately at the antics of a fifth rate clown, or gaping at the Punch and Judy show, or dancing together around the old fiddler sitting on the ground, or throwing the "Knock 'em downs" or bowling at the milky cocoa-nuts, was an offence to those who affected a superiority of taste. They did not like the noise of the crowd . . . it is nothing but a drunken rowdy show, a public pest, and a nuisance. So in time, for one cause and another, the old sports fell away.

By 1911 there were twice as many gamekeepers as rural policemen. The poacher and the gamekeeper often came into conflict. Why do you think the dog is muzzled?

THE SHOOT

In *Winter Harvest* (1967) Michael Home described why organised shoots were so popular, not only with those who took part.

> Even at an ordinary shoot, every available man and boy would be needed as brushers or to go on Stop. A brusher is a beater. A boy on stop was expected to turn the game back to the guns. A man not only got more than his ordinary wage and in far less time, but was also given a free lunch. A boy was paid a shilling. It was that enormous sum, and the fact that the lunch was called a beef lunch, that attracted me.

The Country School

Many of the country schools in the nineteenth century were very small, and would be the only school many children would attend. Several had only one teacher, who would live in the school house which was attached to the school. By the end of the century most teachers had been trained, but this was not always so. Most parents paid a few pence each week for their children's schooling. It did not become free until 1891. Schooling was made compulsory in 1880, but only in 1893 was the leaving age set at 11.

THE DAME SCHOOLS

In the early years the worst schools were run by people who had no qualifications and little education. A School Inspector described Dame schools in Gloucestershire to the House of Commons Committee on Education in 1837:

> **The teachers generally speaking, are totally unqualified, very few, if any, have ever had any education for the purpose. A great proportion of them have undertaken it in consequence of distress, and also because they are**

GOING TO SCHOOL IN HUNTINGDONSHIRE

Sybil Marshall's father started school just before five years of age in the 1870s. The school, in Huntingdonshire, was supported by the Fellowes Family, but a penny a week was charged. His recollections are included in Sybil Marshall's book, *Fenland Chronicle* (1967):

> **When I was nearly five I started going to school, to a place three miles away. This was a terrible drag for us little 'uns to walk, especially in winter. We had to take our dockey [lunch] and were gone all day long; sometimes in the winter it 'ould be pitch dark afore we got home.**

> **getting too old for anything else. The masters and mistresses are generally obliged to follow other occupations for a living. In one instance a woman was washing while she was teaching the children.**

Why do you think parents sent children to schools like this?

Schoolchildren at Astley Village School in 1899. The village had a population of only 331 in 1871. Note the dirty smocks worn by some of the children.

... The school had children from two villages which were divided by a bridge over the river, a tributary of the Nene. The school stood next to the bridge and atween the youngsters from the two villages a bitter feud raged.

... Attendance at the school warn't compulsory and all the summer months the older boys from our side o' the bridge had to stop at home and go a-weeding or some such work in the fields.

At which other times of the year do you think attendance was low?

HOCKHAM CHURCH SCHOOL, SUFFOLK IN THE 1890s

In *Winter Harvest* Michael Home complained about the Mathematics which he believed was not relevant to the rural child. Do you agree?

The teaching of arithmetic was a matter of a book with problems and answers ... in the upper classes [forms], we had to work out how long it would take two men to empty a cistern or the exact spot where two trains would meet after starting at certain speeds from different stations. Children all over the country were doing that. The system took no heed of the fact that we were a farming community. A lot of a labourer's work was piece work, but there wasn't a single man in the village who knew how to work it out, even roughly, the acreage of a field.

SCHOOL OUTINGS

The headteacher was required to keep a daily diary or log. The log of Boughton Monchelsea Primary School, Kent, was published by the school in 1963 to commemorate their Anniversary. Here are some entries.

June 23, 1874. Excursion [to the Crystal Palace] took place today. The Master, two Pupil Teachers and 78 children all thoroughly enjoyed the day and with the exception of one or two over-fatigued headaches everything was a success. All arrived at Boughton at 12 o'clock at night.

June 30, 1874. The master gave a treat to children who did not go to the Palace. After leaving school in the afternoon all the little ones sat down to a comfortable tea ... after amusing themselves in Pond Field, each child had a toy and some sweets to go home with.

Aug. 17, 1877. School Treat given to-day by the Master. The children (221) assembled at the school at 3 o'clock, proceeded at once to Pond Field, (kindly lent by Mr. Skinner) and after enjoying Aunt Sally, Coco Nut Throwing, Donkey Riding, swinging etc. they returned to a good tea at 5 o'clock. After eating and drinking something, grace was sung and before leaving every child had a present. The happy party finished the entertainment with Fireworks about 9 o'clock and I have every reason to believe all were well satisfied.

Schools like this were well run. Have you a village school? Try to find out when it was built and whether the log books have been preserved.

Budgets and Diets

For much of the century there were more workers than jobs in the countryside. Many families migrated to the towns in search of work, whilst others emigrated to Canada, Australia or New Zealand. For those who remained, especially in the remote areas, times were hard and wages low. Many labourers were paid for the work done or by the day and thus got nothing when they were ill or when the weather was bad. Those who could not manage had to rely on charity or enter the workhouse.

SHOPPING IN THE 1840s

M. Sturge Gretton in *A Corner of the Cotswolds in the Nineteenth Century* (1914) described how the money earned by Oxfordshire farm labourers in the 1840s was spent:

The labourers' wives' shopping in those days was in tiny quantities. A ½d. candle . . . ¼oz. of tea, ¼lb. of sugar, ¼lb. of cheese, with some treacle – this would be a typical cottage woman's order repeated three times a week if the husband were in full work. Butter was not bought by the labourers then. Milk he could hardly obtain; morning and night in the cottages the kettle broth was much in evidence. This was composed of a thick slice of stale bread broken into a basin, with a lump of dripping, pepper and salt, and hot water poured over it.

A SUFFOLK BUDGET 1843

Here is the weekly budget of an agricultural labourer of Lavenham, Suffolk in 1843:

Name	Age	Earnings	
		s.	d.
Robert Crick	42	9.	0
Wife	40		9
Boy	12	2.	0
,,	11	1.	0
,,	8	1.	0
Girl	6		–
Boy	4		–
Total earnings		13.	9

Expenditure

	s.	d.
Bread	9.	0
Potatoes	1.	0
Rent	1.	2
Tea		2
Sugar		3½
Soap		3
Blue		½
Thread, etc.		2
Candles		3
Salt		½
Coal and Wood		9
Butter		4½
Cheese		3
	13.	9

(J. Burnett, *Plenty and Want*, 1966)

What is entirely missing from the diet? What would happen if one of the wage earners were ill?

A FOREMAN IN 1892

Edward Wood was a foreman in Bromyard, Herefordshire, and his budget was used as evidence in *The Royal Commission Report on the Agricultural Labourer* (1893-94).

The family – Man, wife, one boy working on a farm, 4 children, 9, 7, 5, 2. (One lad at service in a gentleman's stable, and two girls in domestic service away from home.)

Wages	£.	s.	d.
Edward Wood		16.	0
Boy		6.	0
	1.	2.	0

One week's expenditure

	s.	d.
11 loaves of bread at 5d.	4.	7
1 quarter of flour		5
7lbs. of meat at 7d.	4.	1
3½lbs. of cheese at 6d.	1.	9
2lbs. of butter at 1/3d.	2.	6
½lb. of tea	1.	0
6lbs. of sugar at 2d.	1.	0
4 packets of cocoa at 2d.		8
2lbs. of rice at 2d.		4
1lb. candles		5
2 quarts of oil for lamp		4½
Club money		11½
	18.	1

One year's clothing, etc.

	£.	s.	d.
7 pairs boots	2.	12.	0
Clothing	3.	0.	0
4 tons of coal at 20/–	4.	0.	0
200 faggots		14.	0
	10.	6.	0

(average of 4/– a week)

N.B. Rent free
Gets coat, pair of trousers from employer at Christmas and cast off dress for children.

What is included in this budget which is absent from the previous one?

Villagers often received help from the richer families. In this photograph from Chelsfield, Kent, the lady from Court Lodge is giving food. Can you identify her? Note that the cottagers are in their best clothes for the photograph.

A BILL OF FARE FOR FORTY PERSONS, 1861

Mrs Beeton's *Book of Household Management* was first published in 1861. It rapidly became a best-seller and was read by many prosperous families. Here is a selection of the items Mrs Beeton recommended for inclusion in a picnic:

A joint of cold roast beef, a joint of cold boiled beef, 2 ribs of lamb, 2 shoulders of lamb, 4 roast fowls, 2 roast ducks, 1 ham, 6 medium sized lobsters, 1 piece of collared calves head, 18 lettuces, 6 baskets of salad, stewed fruit . . . 3 or 4 dozen plain pastry biscuits to eat with stewed fruit, 2 dozen fruit turnovers, 4 dozen cheese cakes, 2 cold cabinet puddings in moulds, and few jam puffs, 1 large cold Christmas pudding (this must be good) . . .

Which types of food are included here which are absent from the previous budgets?

Transport

The success of the Liverpool to Manchester Railway in 1830 led to much railway building and by 1850 the main framework of the railways had been completed. Many country stations were built, but many villages were still isolated and goods, crops and people had to travel by road. Carriers with their carts and wagons were the main link between villages and between town and country. Thus, throughout the century, the horse continued to play a major part.

BEFORE THE RAILWAY CAME

The station at Chislehurst, Kent, was not opened until 1865. Before that the nearest station was at Greenwich, some seven miles away. The Reverend Canon Murray gave his recollections in Webb's *History of Chislehurst* (1899):

> **When I came to Chislehurst in 1846, the only and usual means of communication with London for the general public was a very poor coach with a pair of horses, driven by a well-remembered man, "Old Gates", running daily from Orpington, through St. Mary Cray and Chislehurst to the Greenwich Railway, returning the same evening. I was glad instead of this to take sometimes the charming walk through what was Kemnal Wood to join a four horse coach in the Foots Cray Road; which ran daily from Maidstone and back. After this, about the years 1852 to 1860, two omnibuses ran daily from Chislehurst to Greenwich and back.**

Use a directory to find out if there were local carrier services to your nearest station which called at the outlying villages.

THE BLACK BOY INN, CHELMSFORD

At the start of the Victorian period coach travel was very common. When the Black Boy inn was pulled down in 1857, the *Ipswich Express* described how busy it had once been:

> **A quarter of a century ago, between 40 and 50 stage coaches passed its door daily, most of which pulled up, if they did not pause to allow the travellers to partake of the provisions made for them, while numberless pairs of post horses stood saddled in its capacious yard.**

Do you know of any coaching inns? If so does the coach yard still remain? Many modern inns and hotels have replaced earlier ones on the same site. Check in a local directory if you believe this to be the case.

The building of the Hull and Barnsley Railway, showing how the railway cut through the countryside.

THE PRESTON AND WYRE RAILWAY

This Lancashire railway was opened on 25 July 1840 and it enabled farmers to send their goods to the large town of Preston. Before that they had been dependent on the smaller markets at Kirkham, Poulton and Garstang. John Porter in *The History of the Fylde of Lancashire,* published in 1876, showed how the passengers and goods increased:

Week ending	Dec. 14th, 1842	911 Passengers	£ 65.10s. 5d.
		Goods	£ 62. 8s. 1d.
			£127.18s. 1d.
Corresponding week	1844	1,601 Passengers	£139. 4s. 6d.
		Goods	£163.18s.11d.
			£303. 3s. 5d.
,,	1846	2,820 Passengers	£243.19s. 0d.
		Goods	£308.18s. 5d.
			£552.17s. 5d.

The "Iron Horse" must have made a great impression on country people used only to slow-moving coaches. Henry Anderton wrote this poem for the opening in 1840:

Some fifty years since and a coach had
    no power,
To move faster forward than six miles
    an hour,
Till Sawney McAdam made highways
    as good,
As paving-stones crushed into little bits
    could.
The coachee quite proud of his horse-
    flesh and trip,
Cried, 'Go it, ye cripples!' and gave
    them the whip,
And ten miles an hour by the help of
    the thong,
They put forth their mettle and
    scampered along.
The Present has taken great strides of
    the Past,
For carriages run without horses at
    last!
These coaches alive go in sixes and
    twelves,
And once set in motion they travel
    themselves!
They'll run thirty miles while I'm
    cracking this joke,
And need no provisions but pump-milk
    and coke!
And with their long chimneys they skim
    o'er the rails,
With two thousand hundred-weight
    tied to their tails!

Why did the railway lead to the decline of the long distance coach trade?

Difficult Words

bine	the slender stem of a hop plant.
calico	a cotton cloth.
c.	*circa* – about.
club money	weekly payments to provide for such things as medical help and funerals in the time before state help.
cob	a mixture of clay and straw for building.
cooper	a man who makes tubs, casks or barrels.
coppice work	work in a wood, regularly cutting down the branches from young trees for use in making hurdles and hoops.
coulter	the iron cutter in front of a ploughshare.
cowl	a cover or vent in an oast house.
dibble	a pointed tool used for making holes for seeds.
farrier	a man who shoes horses.
four-tined	four-pronged.
gleaning	gathering in seed missed by the reapers.
Hall-boy	boy working in a Hall or great house.
litany	a prayer.
livery	uniform worn by servants in large houses.
lockout	where the worker is stopped from working by his employer.
mounting post	a block or a stone to enable one to mount a horse.
oast house	a kiln where hops are dried.
pale cleaver	hatchet used to split wood for fence palings.
O.S.	Ordnance Survey.
patten maker	a clog maker.
piece work	work paid for by the piece, not by time.
sawyer	one who saws timber.
scullery	a room for kitchen work.
shock	or *stook* – propped-up group of sheaves.
singling	separating.
squire	an English gentleman.
station	one's place.
turnkey	an assistant jailer.
twitching	weeding a very troublesome weed.
wattle and daub	branches daubed or plastered with mud and used as a building material.
wood broker	one who deals in wood.

Money

There were 12 old pence (d.) in a shilling (s.) and 20 shillings in a pound (£). A shilling is equal to 5p.

Prices seem very low, but remember that wages were too. Don't compare prices with those of today, without looking at earnings then and now.

Places to Visit

1. Market towns and villages

a) If you live in, or near a market town, find out whether the market area is still used, on which day the market is held, and what type of market was held in the nineteenth century.

b) *Inns* Were your local inns important as coaching inns, or were they built as the town or village expanded with the coming of the station? Inn signs are useful clues and the older coaching and station yards are well worth a visit.

c) *The church or chapel* Look at memorials and gravestones. Was there previously a gallery in the church, and do any box pews remain? How many stained glass windows date from Victorian times?

d) *Barns and farm buildings* Many model farms were constructed, and an increasing number of buildings were made of brick. They often contain a stone or plaque giving the date or initials of the owner. Sometimes we see "V.R." and the date. Some of the buildings may no longer be used for their original purpose and many of the large barns where winter activities, such as threshing, were pursued now contain machinery and farm implements.

e) *Estate villages* (see pages 10-11) These are easily recognized because they look all of a piece, with the cottages, a school and even church often built at roughly the same period.

f) *Oast houses* Several of these are now being converted into houses. The best examples are in Kent and Sussex.

2. The fields themselves

a) The landscape itself is constantly evolving and in each year many miles of hedgerows are being ploughed up so that machinery can work in larger fields. Compare the fields today with those on a nineteenth-century O.S. map.

b) Even in built-up areas former field boundaries and footpaths across them can be seen by comparing old and new maps. Road names such as Normoss Road, Blowing Sands Road, Highfield Road, Peddars Lane, New Farm Road all remind us of the countryside.

3. Museums

The following list of museums is a selection only and a full list will be found in *Museums and Galleries in Great Britain and Ireland*.

Acton Scott Working Farm Museum, Wenlock Lodge, Acton Scott, near Church Stretton, Shropshire – working horses and farm machinery.

Calderdale Museums, West Yorkshire, includes Ryburn Farm Museum, Ripponden – a typical nineteenth-century Pennine hill farm.

Cirencester, Gloucestershire, Smerrill Farm Museum (between Kemble and Cirencester) – large collection of life in the Cotswolds (1840 – 1940).

Glastonbury, Somerset, Somerset Rural Life Museum. Displays include one on the life of the Victorian farmworker.

Isle of Man, the Cregneash Folk Museum near Port St. Mary – group of furnished cottages, and workshops.

The Grove Rural Life Museum, near Ramsey – large Victorian house with outbuildings.

Lincoln, Museum of Lincolnshire Life – life over the past 200 years.

Reading, Museum of English Rural Life (University of Reading) – an important collection, including a major photographic record.

St. Fagans, South Glamorgan, Welsh Folk Museum. Displays include reconstructed cottages, furnished as they would have been.

Stowmarket, Suffolk, Museum of East Anglian Life – A large open-air museum, which includes working machinery.

Ulster Folk and Transport Museum, Belfast – contains many aspects of the Victorian countryside.

Weald and Downland Museum, Singleton, Sussex. An open air museum which includes a charcoal burner's hut and has several craft demonstrations and many reconstructed buildings.

Biographical Notes

EVANS, George Ewart. He interviewed many country people and his books vividly describe life in East Anglia from the 1880s. He has done much to show the importance of the interview to the historian. He was one of the first to illustrate the value of oral history.

HARDY, Thomas (1840-1928). He was born at Dorchester, in Dorset and wrote many novels set in Wessex (south west England). His books contain much detail of the Victorian countryside and market towns of Dorset.

KILVERT, Robert Francis. He was born in Wiltshire in 1840. In 1865 he went to Clyro in Wales where he was curate for seven years. He kept a diary for nine years. It was closely written in 22 notebooks, and if published in full would fill nine volumes.

MURRAY, John. A famous Victorian publisher whose detailed red guides were often copied but rarely bettered. They were produced for each county, and were frequently revised.

THOMPSON, Flora. She was born in an Oxfordshire village in 1877 and has described her early life in *Lark Rise*, published in 1939. This was followed by *Over to Candleford* (1941) and *Candleford Green* (1943). This trilogy, published as *Lark Rise to Candleford,* vividly describes country life in the 1870s and 1880s.

Book List

The Book List is in two sections. In the first are listed some useful modern books. The second section contains a selection of the books from which extracts were taken for this book.

Modern books

1. Shire Publications have two interesting series:
a) "Shire Albums" which are 32-page books on topics such as old *Farm Tools;* old *Farm Buildings; Fields, Hedges and Ditches; The Village Wheelwright and Carpenter.*
b) "History in Camera" series, e.g. *Hops and Hop Picking* by Richard Filmer. These are over twice the length and more detailed.

2. *Museum Guides and pamphlets* Look out for these in the museums you visit. Excellent examples include the guide to the Weald and Downland Museum (there is a children's guide as well) and the guide to the National Museum of Wales at St Fagans. Pamphlets by the latter museum include one on *The Denbigh Cockpit and Cockfighting in Wales* by I.C. Peate.

3. *Photographic Collections. A Country Camera 1844 – 1914* by A. Winter (Penguin 1973) and the Batsford *Victorian and Edwardian* series contain not only splendid original photographs, but also very useful notes.

Sources of Extracts

1. *Directories, Guides and Gazetteers:*
Kelly's *P.O. Directory of Kent* (1870), Knight's *Suffolk Almanack* (1875), Lewis, *Topographical Dictionary* (1833), Murray's *Devon and Cornwall* (1851 and 1871), Thorne's *Environs of London* (1878), Wilson's *Gazetteer of England and Wales (1876).*

2. *Autobiographies* (published), *diaries and collections of interviews:*
Burnett, J., *Destiny Obscure* (1982), *Useful Toil* (1974)
Marshall, S., *Fenland Chronicle* (1967)
Evans, G.E., *Where Beards Wag All* (1970)
Evans, G.E., *The Farm and the Village* (1969)
Plomer, W. (ed.), *Kilvert's Diary* (1964)
Thompson, F., *Lark Rise to Candleford* (1937)

3. *Detailed studies:*
Horn, P., *Labouring Life in the Victorian Countryside* (1976)
Samuel, R. (ed.), *Village Life and Labour* (1975)
Mingay, G.E., *The Victorian Countryside* (2v) (1981)

4. *Original materials,* e.g. Census returns and Royal Commission material.

Index

accounts:
    country house 15
    repairs and additions 17

Bampton 6
bark strippers 22, 23
Beeton (*Book of Household Management*) 41
blacksmith 32
Boughton Monchelsea 39
Bromley 22, 23, 29, 31
budgets:
    agricultural labourer 40
    country house owner 15
    foreman 41

Carshalton 9
census material 5, 14, 18, 33
charcoal burners 23
Chelmsford 42
Chelsfield 9, 41
children's work:
    crow scaring 27
    field work 24
    hall boy 14, 27
    leading horses 27
    straw plaiting 33
    year's work 26
Chislehurst 35, 42
church:
    music 19
    vicar 18
cottages:
    condition 4, 13
    estate 10, 11
    overcrowding 12
    water supply 13
country crafts 32, 33
country house 14, 15
country town 6, 7
cycle of work 26

Darrington 34
Day, A.C. 21, 30
diaries 19, 24, 36

directories 6, 9
Dugdale, T. 7

East Harting 9
emigration 3
estate owners 16, 17
Evans, G.E. 32, 33

farming jobs 20
farm servants 21

gamekeepers 37
Gangs Act 1867 24
Government Reports 10, 24, 25, 41

Haddenham 31
hall boy 14
Hardy, T. 22, 34, 35
harvest 30, 31
Helmingham 10, 11
hiring fair 34, 35
Hockham 39
Home, M. 9, 19, 37
hops and hop-picking 28, 29
Horley 35
Hugesson, E.K. 36

inns 34

Jefferies, R. 16, 30
Jekyll, Mrs 13

Kelly, *Post Office Directory* 9
Kilvert, R.F. 19
Knight, *Suffolk Almanack* 6

labour book 16, 20, 28
labourers' dress 21
log book 25, 39

markets 6, 7
Marshall, S. 21, 38, 39
Munby, A.J. 24
Murray, J., *Guide to Devonshire* 12

Netley Hall 17

oast houses 29
oral interviews 20, 21
Orpington 18, 22

peat carrying 20
Penshurst 29
ploughman 20
poaching 27
poster (fair) 35
Preston Hall 15
Preston and Wyre Railway 43

railway station 7, 9
Rainham 8
Rider Haggard 13
Rugby 7
rural gangs 24, 25

sawyer 22, 23, 32, 33
schools:
    dame 38
    church 38, 39
    outings 39
Shrublands Hall 14
songs (hiring) 35

Taine, H. 12
Thame 7
Thompson, F. 11, 12
Thorne, J. 8, 9
Tollemache 10, 11
turf digging 21

viaduct 5
villages 8, 9, 10, 11

Warde, Norman 16, 17
Washington 8
wells 13
wheelwrights 32, 33
Wickham Market 6
Willesden 9
Wilson, J. 6
woodmen 22, 23